Amazing Military Vehicles

MILITARY TANKS
IN ACTION

Kay Jackson

PowerKiDS press

New York

To Aden

Published in 2009 by The Rosen Publishing Group, Inc.
29 East 21st Street, New York, NY 10010

First Edition

Editor: Nicole Pristash
Book Design: Julio Gil
Photo Researcher: Jessica Gerweck

Photo Credits: Cover, pp. 5, 13, 14 Courtesy of the Department of Defense; pp. 6, 9, 10, 18, 21 © Getty Images; p. 17 © AFP/Getty Images.

Library of Congress Cataloging-in-Publication Data

Jackson, Kay.
  Military tanks in action / Kay Jackson. — 1st ed.
    p. cm. — (Amazing military vehicles)
  Includes index.
  ISBN 978-1-4358-2749-3 (library binding) — ISBN 978-1-4358-3159-9 (pbk.)
ISBN 978-1-4358-3165-0 (6-pack)
  1. Tanks (Military science)—Juvenile literature. I. Title.
  UG446.5.J23 2009
  623.7'4752
                                    2008033672

Manufactured in the United States of America

CONTENTS

Tanks

When the U.S. military needs to push through enemy lines, the military brings in tanks. Because of a tank's heavy **armor**, **bullets** and even **missiles** have a hard time stopping a tank.

The tracks on a tank allow it to race across a desert, push through woods, or move over blown-up buildings. Tanks often take the lead during battle, and their large guns clear the way for ground forces.

Tanks do not work alone, though. Tanks roll alongside troops while trucks follow behind with tools. Helicopters tell tank commanders where enemy tanks are hiding, too. Tanks are part of a team.

The U.S. military uses tanks every day around the world. This tank and its crew are working in Iraq.

This picture shows a U.S. Army tank patrolling the streets of Cologne, Germany, in 1945, during World War II.

War Tanks

Tanks were first used in World War I. During the war, soldiers hid in **trenches** on the battlefield, but the enemy often kept the soldiers from leaving the trenches. Tanks, however, could cross the field and wipe out the enemy and their guns. Tanks also had an important part in World War II. Tanks had become faster and more powerful, and radios helped tank commanders talk with other tank crews.

Today's tanks are packed with **technology**. **Digital** cameras let the tank's driver see what is outside. Computers connect tanks together and figure out where to aim the big guns.

Tracks of Steel

Tanks are military **vehicles** with steel tracks. Tracks allow a tank's weight to be spread out evenly, so a tank can easily move over soft dirt. Tracks give tanks good **traction**.

Vehicles with four wheels touch the ground in four spots, but tanks with tracks touch the ground in many spots. Having tracks is like having hundreds of fingers digging at once. Tracks allow tanks to easily climb over steep hills.

Tracks can also climb over things that would stop regular wheels. When a tank meets a log or a big rock, the tracks go up and over them.

The tracks on this tank are pushing the tank forward so it can knock down an enemy building. Soldiers can then enter the building safely.

Tanks are used in battle, but tanks are also used to make sure fighting does not happen. This Army tank is keeping watch on a street in Iraq.

First into Battle

Tanks are an important part of the U.S. Army and the Marines. Both branches have small, light tanks and large main battle tanks. The Army and the Marines use tanks in the same way. Tanks are first into a battle.

Tanks can help U.S. forces take over towns or parts of a country. If the enemy is hiding in a building, a tank's powerful gun can tear the building down. Tanks are put in front of ground troops, and they can clear out land mines. Tanks can also stop enemy convoys. Convoys are long lines of vehicles.

A Tank's Metal Shell

Tanks have an outer covering of metal armor. Like a turtle's shell, the armor wraps all around the tank to keep its crew safe from danger.

Some of today's armor is made up of **layers** of metal, plastic, **ceramics**, and even air. This armor can stop missiles. When a missile hits a tank covered with this armor, the first ceramic layer breaks up into fast-moving pieces. The pieces stop the missile head from going through the rest of the tank's armor.

Some new armor even explodes when it gets hit with a missile. The armor then pushes the missile away.

A tank has a hatch, or door, that keeps its crew safe when the hatch is closed. This crew member is using a tank's hatch to see outside.

Here you can see a U.S. Marine tank firing a powerful round out of its main gun during a training exercise in Virginia.

Big Guns, Little Guns

A modern tank has a large main gun. The main gun is about 4 inches (100 mm) wide. The gun is mounted on a tank's **turret**, which can turn to face all directions. When the enemy is spotted, the turret spins around to face the enemy. The big gun fires High Explosive Anti-Tank, or HEAT, rounds. These rounds can often go right through an enemy tank's armor.

Tanks also have smaller guns. Usually, a large machine gun and two smaller guns are mounted on the turret. The machine guns are fired at enemy trucks, planes, and buildings.

High Technology

Tanks are more than just guns and armor, though. Tanks are machines with tons of technology. Tank commanders and drivers look through digital **periscopes** that can see through darkness, dust storms, and smoke. A computer figures out how far away a **target** is. Then, the computer sets the height of the main gun and where the gun is pointed. With this system, tanks can fire while moving.

Modern tanks have powerful engines. Tanks can drive down a road at 45 miles per hour (72 km/h). This is very fast since a tank can weigh 60 tons (54 t) or more!

This Army soldier is controlling one of the guns inside his tank. Technology has made guns very exact, and soldiers can aim the guns better.

The M-1 Abrams tank is counted on by the military to do its most important jobs. This M-1 Abrams tank is clearing the way for other forces to come through.

The Main Battle Tank

The U.S. Army and the Marines' main battle tank is the M-1 Abrams. The M-1 Abrams tank can fight in any weather. Uneven ground, big rocks, and deep trenches do not stop the Abrams.

Computers have made big changes in main battle tanks. Older tanks once used radios to talk with other tanks, but tank crews were often cut off from other crews on the battlefield. Today, technology allows the M-1 Abrams to get reports from other tanks as well as from helicopters, planes, and ground troops. Computer screens show where enemy tanks are and where other U.S. tanks are.

Tank Crews

Tank crews generally have four people in them. Each member has a job. The tank commander decides the tank's direction and when to fire the guns. The driver drives the tank and uses three periscopes to see out of the tank. The loader puts shells into the main gun. The gunner fires the machine guns.

Tank crews train together. First, they learn battlefield plans, drills, and how tanks work. Then, the crew trains in a simulator, which is a room that is set up like the inside of a tank. At last, the crew trains inside a real tank.

This soldier is working on one of the tracks on his tank. Tank crew members often know how to fix tanks in case one breaks down.

An Uncertain Tomorrow

Tanks and their crews are a valued part of the U.S. military. For nearly 100 years, military commanders and troops have depended on tanks. However, tanks may not be around forever.

Some people say that tanks are not needed anymore. Some believe that tanks are too big and they are spotted too easily. However, others say that tanks are here to stay. New kinds of armor are making tanks lighter. New computer systems are making tanks a part of everything that happens on the battlefield. One thing is for certain, though. Tanks are an important part of the military because they help keep troops safe.

Glossary

armor (AR-mer) A hard cover put over something to keep it safe.

bullets (BU-lets) Things that are shot out of a gun.

ceramics (suh-RA-miks) Matter that is heated until it hardens.

digital (DIH-juh-tul) A form of words, pictures, and sound that is readable by a computer.

layers (LAY-erz) Thicknesses of something.

missiles (MIH-sulz) Objects that are shot at something far away.

periscopes (PER-uh-skohps) Tools that are used to see above the tops of tanks.

target (TAR-git) Something that is aimed at.

technology (tek-NAH-luh-jee) The way people do something and the tools they use to do it.

traction (TRAK-shun) The grip a moving object has on a surface.

trenches (TRENCH-ez) Long pits dug in the ground where soldiers hide to shoot at an enemy.

turret (TUR-et) A round object with guns mounted on it that can spin.

vehicles (VEE-uh-kulz) Means of moving or carrying things.

Index

A
armor, 4, 12, 15–16, 22

B
battle, 4, 11
building(s), 4, 11, 15

C
commander(s), 4, 7, 16, 20, 22

F
forces, 4, 11

G
gun(s), 4, 7, 11, 15–16, 20

H
helicopters, 4, 19

M
military, 4, 22
missile(s), 4, 12

P
periscopes, 16, 20

T
technology, 7, 16, 19
tracks, 4, 8
traction, 8
trenches, 7, 19
troops, 4, 11, 19, 22
trucks, 4, 15
turret, 15

W
woods, 4
World War I, 7

Web Sites

Due to the changing nature of Internet links, PowerKids Press has developed an online list of Web sites related to the subject of this book. This site is updated regularly. Please use this link to access the list:

www.powerkidslinks.com/amv/tanks/